THE MEAN GAME

THE MEAN GAME

John Wall Barger

Palimpsest Press
1171 Eastlawn Ave.
Windsor, Ontario. N8S 3J1
www.palimpsestpress.ca

Printed and bound at Coach House Printing in Ontario, Canada.
Book design by Dawn Kresan. Edited by Jim Johnstone.

Cover art by Paul Klee. Front cover: "Adam and Little Eve" (1921).
Back cover: "Where Eggs and the Good Roast Come From" (1921).

Palimpsest Press would like to thank the Canada Council for the Arts
and the Ontario Arts Council for their support of our publishing
program. We also acknowledge the assistance of the Government of
Ontario through the Ontario Book Publishing Tax Credit.

LIBRARY AND ARCHIVES CANADA CATALOGUING IN PUBLICATION

TITLE: The mean game / John Wall Barger.
NAMES: Barger, John Wall, 1969– author.
DESCRIPTION: Poems.
IDENTIFIERS: Canadiana (print) 2019004506x
            Canadiana (ebook) 20190045078

ISBN 9781989287095 (SOFTCOVER) | ISBN 9781989287118 (EPUB)
| ISBN 9781989287101 (PDF) | ISBN 9781989287132 (KINDLE)
CLASSIFICATION: LCC PS8603.A734 M43 2019 | DDC C811/.6—DC23

CONTENTS

The failure of love might count for most of the suffering in the world.
—MARIE HOWE

The master said *You must write what you see.*
But what I see does not move me.
The master answered *Change what you see.*
—LOUISE GLÜCK

Urgent Message from the Captain of the Unicorn Hunters

Release them. Those sealed in your attics.
Those chained in your barns. Those on the nightmare yokes.
Those heads on your walls. This is our fault.
We taught you to torture the unicorn.
That it biteth like a lion & kicketh like a horse.
That it has no fear of iron weapons.
That unicorn-leather boots ensure sound legs
& protection from plague. That unicorn liver (with a paste
of egg yolk) heals leprosy. That its tusk,
ground to dust, makes men hard. Forget all that.
Taxidermists, lay down your saws.
Keep off, ye farmers of dreams & horns.
We have done enough. Baiting them with our virgins.
Cutting the heads off the calves & their mothers.
Planting birthday candles in their eyes.
Fortune-telling with their gizzards.
Tossing their balls to the dogs.—Enough!
Free them to bathe in our rainbows.
Let them loose in their fields of sorrow.
Enough have they tholed. And you'll have to forgive:
nothing that's happened as yet
has prepared me for this. I have taken us too far
off course. Abominations, treason!
It's up to them now, our lot.
First, *let them go*. And then we wait.

Your Suitors

Like fast clouds they creep in.
They seem to know where you are headed,
like family dogs. They storm the restaurant where we eat
wearing coffee cups & legs of lamb.
Do your suitors ever sleep? They seem to wake up
drunk. They withdraw as one, like deer. As if running for a bus
but there is no bus. All speaking at once
like a suicidal teen. Your suitors form a hanging wall
around your beauty. On street corners they slouch,
hardly breathing. They fog in like sharks
to our corner of the party. They shark in like fog, as if dancing
but they are not dancing. As if drowning.
Don't get me wrong, I wouldn't change a thing.
At karaoke they are lovely. Kind, even.
They anticipate your joy as if they'd loved you
an eternity. Even as you fall on me
I feel their proximity. That they too are naked.
As naked as that tree across the street, before a snowstorm.
That maple which is probably dying.

The Wonderful Hat

Slurred Dziengielewski, "We're all of us ants in a sugar bowl, bro."
I raised my jam jar of tequila to that. June bugs collided against
the windows like tiny warplanes. We were having a splendid night.
Dziengielewski was in fine form, raving in his armchair. "Ol' pal, I
had a vision of a past life," he said. "I jumped off a bridge for love.
My very last thought was, what a shame to ruin my wonderful hat!"
"What wonderful hat?" I asked. "One of those stovepipe hats made of
beaver fur." "Do you have such a hat?" "I do not." He looked at me in
triumph. After this I found it hard to keep track of the conversation.
While sipping tequila & chuckling at jokes, I imagined touching &
smelling the stovepipe hat. It was brown, shiny, tattered, stray threads
poking out, with a black sash, & a dime-sized hole on top. The kind of
hat that makes you look & feel like a million bucks. It never existed,
though I seemed to remember it. I bid Dziengielewski adieu with a
tip of the unreal hat. Driving at night in the rain, I yawned. There
was roadkill everywhere. I shut my eyes & their eyes rolled open. I
pulled over to clear my thoughts, stepping out into the fall air, the faint
weight of the hat on my head. All was still, even the rain. The bright
drops hovered, like a photo of snow, like stars. Up & down the road,
small bodies rose heavily to their feet.

The Stiltwalkers

We arrived on horseback. The locals
pooled around us, faces kind & open.
They brought us parrots, balls of cotton.
They were well-built with good bodies.
We poisoned the water. Burned the temples.
They had been rich in materials.
We designed their poverty from scratch.
Poured wine on each other's beards,
laughing, dubbing ourselves kings.
Introduced a law: the feet of each local
would be severed & upon each stump
a tall wooden stilt be sewn,
so they could not escape the woods.
They turned on us. My comrades fled.
I locked myself in the palace.
Their stilts on the gravel at midnight
were thunder. I escaped to the brink of a deep barranca
singing my death chant & hurled myself in.
I survived. Now I walk among them, disguised
as an old woman, feet strapped to stilts,
ankles blistered, toes smashed. They eye me
at market, but I do not break. I hobble to my room
under the stairs. Peel off my mask & wool dress.
O, freedom becomes them. They have grown eloquent
in walking. Running faster than we ever could.
Tall as birches. Their young born
stilted. I hear their voices, drowning phonemes,
through the floors. I do not make a sound.
I am afraid to look, but at night I peek out
at their dances. They lope like puppets

& never fall. Women gyrate in a ring around the bonfire.
Behind, the men jump, ever higher, calling for love.
Women catch them. Everyone begins to spin,
these giants, arms upraised, slowly, then blurring—
impossibly—& sing in a collective low
moan the joy of their dark hearts like gods.

The Problem with Love

My brother died & I got his tarantula.
Ma asked if I was fucking man enough
& I said "Yeah" so she handed me a book,
*Tarantulas, Their Captive Husbandry
& Reproduction*, & went back to her TV shows.
It was a girl spider. She lived in a fish tank
with plastic ferns & a tiny house
just big enough to hide in.
She let me hold her & she never bit.
She spun a silk forest to decorate her house.
I fed her bugs & told her tales
I made up about Pa. I came in the room
& she rattled her little pedipalp hands,
which they do when mating,
hoping I'd pick her up. One day
she fell off my arm onto the floor
& just lay there a second
before creeping toward her fish tank,
& one of her legs fell off.
I placed her in, gently.
She crawled, wonky, into her house.
I had a bad dream that night.
I woke in the dark, found Ma's hair scissors,
reached into the spider's house
& cut off a leg. She hissed at me
& hid. Next morning she wobbled
out to greet me, & I cut off another leg.
Each day I cut another leg.
She stopped spinning a silk forest.
Her legs grew back

& I just cut them off again.
Soon she wouldn't come out
of her house, or eat her crickets.
She tossed sharp hairs at me,
teeny spears. Then her legs
did not grow back. She sat in her house,
gray, hissing like a punctured
basketball. One morning
I scooped her into my palm,
chatting like the old days
& she just sat there, not biting.
In the backyard I lowered her
onto an anthill. As the red ants
climbed her, swarmed & lynched her,
I hosed down the fish tank.
It took ten minutes to scrub it
spotless, so the sun
really shone through the glass.

At the Front

Buses drove us to the patriotic camps
where we learned
to mortify the flesh
& slay the savage Abbieannians
before they slayed us.
Helicopters lowered us
to a dry & fireless camp
& flew away. The front.
A great wind rushed
under us. We marched
into the dense smoke,
weapons drawn, as taught.
There at last we faced
our enemies, the Abbieannians.
They waved to us
across a maze of trenches.
We laid our guns down
& sat with them in the grass
beside a river
that cried like a human.
They met us with courtesy
always. We traded stories.
Their language was different (*bird*
for *god, love* for *bread*)
but the meaning
was the same. Inevitably,
we switched sides.
We made them maps
to our gold. They offered keys
to their houses.

They explained how to run
their family businesses.
We shook hands
& crossed their border.
We wept when we left
the front. It was the best place
we'd ever been.

Ash Baptism

I was nine when the ash
drifted to our flatlands
like a mountain.
Our farms stood on hind legs,
staggered to the coast.
We stayed, eating our bellies out.
Shooting cattle, landholders.
Living inside the ash,
the cave of it. Citizens of it,
believers. Father,
thinking as it thought,
chewed dead grass
in the yard. Father bleated.
Mother squatted naked in the road.
Mother cawed.
Ash a church in the sky.
We hacked out prayers
on the rocks & trees of it,
delivered from the bondage of the sun
& its unchaste burning.
Ash galloped off
with our small ones
to the afterworld. We offered it
everything. On the Sabbath,
starving, staggering,
I held forth my last Twinkie
to the swirling.
There came a wind,
shapes. A black spark,

an inkling—past & future among
like fallen statuary.
The monkeys stood
waist-deep. The largest,
The Grand Seigneur,
wore a sleazy grin.
Eyes gray, mouth gray.
"Let every living soul
prosper," he grunted.
"The Twinkie in your claw,"
I said, "is that the soul?"
He placed his bloodflecked crown
on my head. "All hail
boy-king," he muttered,
grinning, in the ash.

A Briefe & Marveyllous Hystory of Franklin

After two years of pregnancy
& the poor lass
had still not given birth
could hardly squeeze through doors
they named the unborn
Franklin & called a sawbones.
The family convened
for dinner at the far edges
of a mahogany table
like opposite shores of a lake
under which at long last
Franklin wriggled free.
Father's soup spoon fell: "Harke yee,
'tis a *hors*," he said.
Yes, Franklin was a black colt.
He stared at them, his family,
his eyes clear as a cave pool.
In their eyes he observed
numberless blossoms or eggs
hatching. Fur slathered
in seaweed of another age,
he wiped his face with a hoof,
he spake: "Semes th' ocean-seas
be wyder yet." In those months
Franklin did not adapt
to the mansion. Did not adore
his big-as-an-equipage
oaken bassinet. Did not love
the hyperactive crosseyed
hound. Even his blood kin

their ringlets their grass stains
their ditties
he could do without.
What he liked was the barn,
its pigs & goats & sheep.
He squirmed out
of the embroidered cardigan
his mother knit.
His favorite bed, dry hay.
He grew colossal, twice any horse
they'd seen. The family,
mistaking his bulk
& his intelligent eyes
for menace, kept their distance.
Said the priest, "Lijk to him
y neuere noon knewe."
Franklin knew which days
were slaughter days.
He knelt in the barn
with each animal
whose morning had come.
Today it is Sally the pig.
He nestles his great black nose
on her belly. He wants
as he always wants
to emancipate them
to lead them to the blue field
he dreamt of. But where is
the blue field? And what then?
To himself he reasons

Be not conformed to this truth
but be ye transformed
by the renewing of—
what? So he consoles Sally
telling her that this life
is a "furyous dræm"
that he'll see her again anon
that she has been chosen
for suffering, which is noble.
Sally blinks. After an hour
he crouches low. Sally steps upon
his back & he walks her
the long way around the pond
as slow as he can.

The Two-Headed House

A man climbs on a woman's back, digs claws
into her sides, pierces her armor & holds on
a lifetime. He sleeps. She drags him along,
licks the length of a grass blade, aches for sweetness.
He waggles his cercus on her ovipositor
which she hardly notices. She halts
under a picnic table, before a crystal ball-sized
bead of Jägermeister. She dips their heads
into it, they sink in golden mud, sharing a reverie:
they are dragonflies skimming a lake
of stained glass at dusk. First chance she gets,
she bites off his head. He hangs on,
headless, evermore. His quiet infuriates.
But on full moons, the evenings he used to sing
the old songs to her, she feels sentimental.
All day she climbs a garage to the eaves.
At dusk, high above the yard, she lets herself teeter
at the edge of missing him.

A Scorneful Image or Monstrus Shape of a Wondrous Strange Fygure, Presentyng the State & Condicion of This Present World, Containing Many of the Moste Sundry Strange Things, Seming Monstrus in Our Eyes & Judgement, Bicause We Are Not Privie to the Reasons of Them, which Includyth Secrets & Wonders of the Worlde of Leda, & Inespeciall the Detestable Sodomye of Leda, that Have Beene Within This Land

Leda, after a swim,
drowsed in the sunlit grass
when over the lake
a storm cloud plunged,
mushrooming, gathering
in folds like a swan,
wings like amputated trees.
Because he was a god
he stepped out of the garden
grown in the shadow
of our resentments:
his tempest body hovering
like a Manhattan-sized
chandelier shimmering
with owls & goblins
& at the center was she herself
—her brightest self,
black hair, eyes furious,
not old not young—
& this gyring swan-
earthquake rumbling
out of the past toward eternity
entered her. The lake-sky
braced on its haunches
& in his thrust the world converged,
tearing her, driving her

into the mud.
Her body held his thunder
the way language holds a flower,
like two sides of one paper,
words bleeding into
each other & his tongue
in its pleasure flicked
& spat an antique rapture.
Her mind in his dimension
collapsed like a burning
house. He withdrew.
A mist rose,
a whispering of all tongues.
That night she scratched
poems till her fingers clenched
in a knot around the pen,
a hurt animal
crawling toward a drop of water.
Her husband
snored loudly.

Voyeur

Czarina, my spyglass is trained on you
while you lie topless in the sun,
reading. Clouds assemble over you
like bored gods. I can make out
the vial of goose grease you smear
on your face. A Persian cat
that resembles a massive dust bunny
sleeps in a basket
under your chaise lounge.
The book you're reading happens to be
one of mine. I try to discern
from your wincing & recoiling
which poem you're on. You laugh—
from joy or cruelty is not clear.
My inventions fill me with shame.
I hate you. A spot of red drifts
into the frame. A fox. Are you asleep?
It hoists your cat into its mouth
& trots away with it.
I want to yell, to warn you
but my wife is napping beside me
under a clean white sheet.
A wind worries the air,
like the out-breath of an extortionist
over the phone, having to explain
yet again what is owed.

The Bureaucrats

We never should have crossbred the bureaucrats with office supplies. "But," you said, "how convenient! With microchip eyes they send emails by winking. With opposable big toes they operate four staplers at once." Soon the bureaucrats could take no more. They escaped our electric fences & fled to the woods. They crossed the burntlands, single file, their young in their teeth. They slept beside coyotes, surviving on power bars, energy drinks, pinecones. Around fires they held workshops on flesh-eating. Their old chieftain died & was reborn as a little girl who they ate. No one could say when or how they came back. One day at the mall there was a bureaucrat chewing a cheeseburger. Another jogged at the gym. Suddenly they were parading down Main, waving soiled neckties attached to Bic pens like flags. Grinning, thumbs up, mouths crusted with blood. And just like that, without fanfare, the bureaucrats were in charge. Now we must answer their questionnaires, without error, to receive permission to sleep & to wake. We must fill out surveys even in our dreams. Penalties—for misspellings, errant paperwork, infractions on the perpetual audits—are swift, severe. Schools are prisons. Hospitals are abattoirs. They wear our scalps as purses. Our spleens, they say, are delicacies. In broad daylight I come across three bureaucrats crouched over a body in the street, feasting on it like starving boars. Leaving no waste.

Undelivered Letter (TO: CAPT. HENRY DARGER, Janitor,
Alexian Brothers Catholic Hospital, Chicago-Land)

This is Hettie Annie. I am small.
Mr. Darger, I write you
of the massacres. We need you.
Glandelinians chain us
to the cedars. We are the last
devotees at Jennie Richee.
We are the child slave rebellion.
Blengigomeneans discard us,
flying off, horns piercing
the sun like winged rhinos.
The ink of wickedness bleeds
on the firmament shell.
Mr. Darger, we can no longer
dance on God's jeweled
dance floor, satchels spilling
roses & ridges & rivers
in the all-day dusk. The crystal forest
freezes our tiny fingers.
Lunatics tie us to birches,
sacrificing us at the sacred yurts.
We lower our pants
before God. My sisters birth
my sisters. The cairn
is regained. Mr. Darger,
I set out for you. I outran arrows,
swam moonlit lakes,
camped haunted moors.
Limped toward you, mapless,
hand on my heart.

Crossed an epoch of woods
till I came to a street.
Clambered toward you
over suburb fences.
A man said he loved me.
I was blindfolded, tied to tables.
Mr. Darger, protector
of children, I think you
have dreamt of me,
where you wash dishes
& roll bandages for God.
I am here, on the sidewalk.
Look out your window.

My Houseguest

I heard sounds, late. Tapping, scratching.
An infestation. Neighbors swore
something stretched out my window
to nibble my lettuce. Each night
faint music. Each morning the same record,
Blind Willie Johnson's *Praise God
I'm Satisfied*, on the turntable.
Livid, I began sleeping with the record
under my pillow. The doorknob
turned in the dark: an orange creature
slithered in, slow, soundless,
neck unfolding like a sorcerer's hand.
A giraffe. She laid her great head
on my lap. "I hoped to meet,"
she said, "before they took me."
I held her. "Stay, please,"
I said. "Keep the Blind Willie.
I'll buy you a slide guitar."
Her milk eyes rolled. "They will ..."
she said, nuzzling my cheek
with a soft ear, "sell my fur
as toilet seat covers.
They will wear me as a hat."
Sirens. Footsteps. Men in uniform
dragged her out by the legs,
bumping her head on the stairs.
I was alone. The objects in my room,
the jade plant, the old red chair,
assumed a wild clarity.
As if nobody was there to see them.

Penitentiary

Flanked by an electric fence on all sides
I wake wearing the ocean.
I was warned not to run down the breezeway
from courtyard to chapel.
Or to stop in the breezeway.
Or to talk shit. Flanked by a freak on all sides
I wake wearing a Lao Tzu smile.
Flanked by forests on all sides—
hills improvising the nightmare woods
—I wake wearing wind for a nose.
At the center of a spinning dial
of cigarettes, under long russet curtains,
none of us seems ready to utter
what? "The heart," blurts out this fellow
carving a stick bird into his arm
with a nail, "is a lovely wingless moth!"
He has won the game I invented just now,
where the talented are free.
The just receive a just reward.
All have a fair shake,
no matter what palace or cave
they crawl out of. In the arena of love.
The mean game.

Tale of the Boy & the Horse Head

In his dream the boy heard
ting-ting—like chains rattled
in lake water: it was the bell
he'd tied to the tail of the horse.
He woke & ran to the field.
Earth turned slow in the dark.
Look, a horse head on grass
like a broken jack-o'-lantern.
No body. The boy lay beside it,
hand on the honeybrown nose.
He did not cry. A voice
in the house was repeating
his name. He lifted the head
by its mane. He staggered.
It was heavier than a full pail
of water. He waded the river.
Its neck bones tore his shoulder.
In the forest, he hoisted it
onto a branch. It stared down,
one ear up, eyes leaking
white pus. He tried to close
its eyes but could not. The dark
made sounds he misunderstood.
He shut his eyes against it.
He spoke the horse's name,
softly, & slept. First light was cold.
The head wore a shy grin
like a scarecrow. Flies crawled
in & out of its nose. The boy
lifted it & walked. His clothes

bloodblack. Look, dead men
& women beside the road.
Oracle fools in their shacks.
He carried the head under
the sun. The burntlands a slash
in the earth. Charred trees
& boulders scattered by gods.
A vulture wheeled. The boy
screamed at it, dryly, dropping
the head. Worms boiled in its nose.
Worms ate its blackberry eyes.
The boy curled in the dirt
& dreamt souls swam from the head
across a channel toward him.
He dreamt it was his father's head.
They had the same greasy hair.
He carried it day & night,
talking to himself—a rasping,
easy to ignore. He collapsed on a hill
above the village of his grand-
mother. The head, its broken teeth
& swollen tongue, mocked him.
A vulture in feather robes, like Solomon
of the Bible, stood on his chest.
Below, in the castiron dawn,
his grandmother touched her head
to the ground.

Hammer

There's nowhere else to look
but at the rock hammer
the man removes from his boot.
I know what he means to do
from the way he places it
on the table. I force myself to see
the ash stubble on his cheek,
the blood on his wrist.
How well placed, all of it.
How beautiful. His drooping lids,
my trembling hand,
this silent windowless room.
Everything belongs.
Even the hammer's shadow,
like the mean little front garden
of an eerie castle.
Even the rhythmic tapping
on the wall, as if a teenage boy
were outside tossing a ball
against it—bored, killing time
before his girl arrived.
She who now walks the fields
toward us, in bare feet.

The Death of Jolly Dolly

Among the auguries & weary lust
of my hospital bed
I saw Jolly Dolly as she never was:
terribly thin, horribly thin.
I staggered to the river, IV tubes
trailing like puppet strings.
There they all were,
heads bowed like bad kids.
Midget City sang a dirge:
"Jolly Dolly's going, going, *gone*
as an old dog bone!"
Pop-eyed Paul caterwauled.
The gravedigger spat,
leaned on his spade.
That's her in the grand piano,
like a newborn elephant
on a cherry parachute.
She who laughed like a burning
bush. She who fell through
the longsuffering floorboards
of her caravan. It took four
to love her, twelve to lower
her sarcophagus. General Gus
spouted the usual crap:
"Forty angels descended
to haul away her lightest self
to that freak show on high ..."
He didn't know her. None of them
did. Tenderhearted, my ass.
Walrus-hearted, more like.

With that straight razor voice
that whittled your soul
to bite-size. But it was starting
to snow & I'd loved her,
so I wished our giantess
a place in a giant land,
where she could feel small.

Prometheus

A glass figurine danced
for the gods, twirling,
reflecting their light
in celestial prisms on the ceiling.
The gods thought
this guy was a blast.
At night he slipped
into their caves
to watch them fuck.
O glory! Like a volcano
boiling, ingesting,
dividing. Like a tree
born in the sun.
His eyes bugged out.
His glass pintle glowed.
The gods, Völundr
& Mahāsthāmaprāpta,
noticed. "Why, a voyeur!"
said Völundr.
They leaned in
as elephants over a worm.
Mahāsthāmaprāpta
grinned. "Give us your eyes,"
she said. "I can't unsee
your splendor,"
said the glass figurine.
"Good answer!"
laughed Völundr,
shattering him with his toe
into a billion shards,

little squidlike beasts,
bald, dripping bile
& mud, cursing light.
They crawled on their bellies
from the mountains
to the valley.
They built a town,
cursing the mountains,
vowing to bore
innumerable holes into them
& through the skulls
of the gods
that didn't want to be friends.

Chernobyl

Annie Edson Taylor
first to survive Niagara Falls in a barrel
she is our heroine.
The Zone glitters like a mirage
an abandoned city
à la Tarkovsky's *Stalker*
fizzing with radiation.
Taylor—praise her—sleepwalks
on the lawn of the soporific
hospital. She blinks,
eyes yellow, shadowed
by the central chimney.
Is it a lighthouse in the desert?
The Zone wears her dream
like a gown. The hospital
wears the rubble like a gown.
Taylor wears a long black dress
& a fruit hat. Front stairs
of the hyperacute hospital,
Taylor coughs, on her knees.
How, you wonder,
did she get here? Don't ask me.
I wanted to write a poem
to exalt a nice thing.
Yet here she is, spasming,
spitting a dark thread.
"Stop!" you say. "Don't go in!"
Yet in she goes.
Her black dress slips off
& her fruit hat. She is naked

walking the hallway
past rooms of box-spring beds.
Here is a room heaped
with clothes: firefighter boots,
gas masks. Sooty tables,
murky slime. An arthritic tree
curls in a shattered window.
A box-spring so tiny
it could be a doll's bed.
Taylor stops, bows low,
palms together, mumbling words
I can't even hear.
I'm tempted to remind her
she died sixty-five years
before Chernobyl.
But now she's alert,
back straight, listening
with her whole body
for what? I beg her
to put on the fruit hat,
just for the end of the poem.
It's not too late!
But she keeps tossing it
onto a pile
of melted toys.

Having Read *The Book of Coming Forth by Day*, I Constructed a Diorama in Hopes that Death Might Visit

I'm reluctant to acknowledge that the diorama was just an empty cardboard box, as my expectations for it were quite high. I'd heard that Death does not accept invitations. Death chooses the time & place. Nevertheless, I waited, fingers crossed. I admit my assumptions—that Death relishes a slow viola, but despises "the human project"—were naïve. I took up smoking. I loved to smoke & stare into the box. One night, sick of the box, I walked to a pub. A real dive. Busted chairs. A drunk dude in sweatpants attempting to dance flamenco. I ordered a beer. The more I drank the better he got. He was mesmerizing. His sweatpants slipped to his knees but he kept on dancing, unfazed, snapping his fingers as if with castanets. When out of nowhere a beer bottle clocked him in the face, something marvelous befell him. His visage twisted, grotesque, as if what terrified him most were happening. His thighs shook, his fingers grasped for the unsayable. Thunder made a seam from the ocean floor to his sneaker, stomping, stomping. On my way home I heard cries in a dumpster. *Mews.* It was a garbage bag of kittens! They peeked out, scared, half-blind. I carried them home & lowered them into the box. I knew I'd keep them. The next day I slathered the box with pink house paint. "Lovely afternoon to start again," I said to the kittens. I flushed my cigarettes down the toilet & resolved never to speak of the deep mysteries, even if one day I learned something about them.

The Headaches

Each is woven with light.
Asylum quilts.
Making me scream
what I'd never speak.
Each a labyrinth
containing one tall, slim, aristocratic
pedophile priest.
Mother left the headaches
without instructions
among the bone china
& souvenir spoons.
I suppose you will think
I am not grateful, Mother.
Each a fingerprint.
Game of some infertile god.
Riddle with a novel way
to wriggle free.
Are you coming back,
Mother? In this new heat
we grow talented.
This person sprouts feathers.
I emit a faint cold gleam
like some blind fish, or movie star.
You should see me.
Faces glow where I walk.
(What awful accumulating
revelation can I be?)
All year it rains.
Tonight, rain on the window

makes the silence
of a finger on a belly.
A new girl has arrived.
I hear her now
washing her armful of flutes
in our bath. I know
she can't stay, Mother.
She has no talent.
But when she plays,
the headaches
curl up on the floor
& shut their eyes like feral cats.

Swarm

Before I meet Angelinia,
the celebrated artist,
my anguish is barbed wire
I am trapped inside.
She shows me the breach.
She is a genius.
I work for her. Welding,
cleaning, painting.
Anything. I obey every prompt,
swallow every pill.
My days have meaning.
I'm vital, she says,
to her process. One Monday
the top of her to-do list
says, "BEST PERFORMANCE EVER!"
I complete it, as usual,
to perfection. At midnight
I enter her bedroom
by the fire escape.
When I'm sure she's asleep
I open the brown bag
marked "SWARM." *Moths fly out.*
Moths spread in a fog,
darkening the walls, windows
&, finally, Angelinia's face
—like a mask of petals,
black petals, plague buboes.
She chokes, dies.
What it means
I don't know. I forget Angelinia.

I move to a tropical
island. The villagers,
called Blengins, accept me.
They're special.
They're small, like dolls.
A full-grown Blengin man
could curl asleep
in your cupped palm.
Their village exists
on one coconut a day.
I swim the green sea.
I eat coconuts.
I live years in harmony
with the Blengins.
One morning as I wake
they are shouting,
pointing at the sea.
I yawn, rub my eyes.
Blengin-sized creatures
are diving out
of coconut shell canoes,
storming the shore.
"Glandelinians! Glandelinians!"
They circle the village,
burning Blengin huts.
I climb a tree.
Glandelinian warriors
pour into the jungle
in black raven wings, howling,
murdering Blengins,

burning all in their path.
When they spot me
they grow quiet.
Two chiefs confer,
standing on the corpses
of the Blengins.
One whispers an order.
The army marches
up the tree, toward me.
The base darkens
with their bodies,
like some grotesque flower
blossoming.

The Confession of Chunosuke Matsuyama

I scratch my tale on strips of wood: *"When I, Chunosuke Matsuyama—now shipwrecked! now starving!—was a boy in Hiraturemura, I met a monk sitting crosslegged, teetering at the edge of a well. 'Whatcha doin'?' I asked. 'Imagining the form of The Problem Solver,' said the monk."* I seal the strips in a bottle. I am so thirsty I lick the glass. I hear a cackle. It is a crow standing in ocean surf. He wears a feather robe. I wade out to show him my bottle. "I put my soul in here," I say. He squints. "That's wood, you halfwit," says the crow. "I'm from a faraway land," I say. "You are cruel & stupid," says the crow. "We came to find a sword." "What sword?" "A one-of-a-kind sword called Little Crow," I say. The crow cackles. "In 150 years," says the crow, "a fisher finds your bottle in the seaweed at Hiraturemura." "Wow!" I say. "I mean," says the crow, "you're more interesting dead." Hearing that, I was enlightened.

The External Lung

The doctors mummified Ezequiel in gauze.
He'd been in a coma
for weeks, chest rising,
falling, ventilator chuffing
like Darth Vader.
External lung, the nurse called it.
I slept on a chair beside Zee
& woke with the lung
looking up at me,
tall as a dehumidifier
or a statuette of Venus.
She had short arms & legs.
In the glass of her chest,
an analog needle, a red light.
Her plastic eyes
blinked. I leaned down
to offer my hand.
She clasped my thumb.
"Shall we," I said,
"take a stroll?" She nodded,
her needle trembling.
We walked streets
Zee & I used to take
smoking & gossiping about girls.
With her mini legs
she could hardly keep up
so I walked slow.
She stopped to offer me a daisy.
"Why thank you," I said.

At the public gardens
she paused. I said,
"Shall we go in?"
She nodded. I hoisted her
over the gate.
We sat in the grass by the lagoon.
A moonless night.
Sleeping ducks
curled on the bank,
feathery loaves of bread.
She climbed on my lap
like an old cat
& shut her eyes. Her red light
flickered, went out.
She let go of my thumb.

Inconceivable Mansion

Walls of the foyer ripple with books
like reptile scales.
Books wordless, preverbal,
sheer verb, prehensile, predatory.
Books under every bed
eat the throats of books.
It's not cruel—books don't think.
The mansion thinks.
The thinking of the mansion
is a dazzling fire in the dining room
where the First Woman,
just born, coughs.
Her first thought, *Kill my sister.*
But she has no sister.
The mansion did not conceive
this First Woman, this stowaway.
She must have climbed
out of a book. The mansion,
furious, rises on the swell of a wave
like a ship on high seas.
The First Woman sinks to mansion bottom.
She steps into a McDonald's.
Presented with such bright
disorienting symbols, she points.
It has been a shitty day.
She slumps over her burger
at a booth beside the ball room
shipwreck. Objects are freed
of utility, unmoored. Kids stare,
eyes eaten by fish.

Amid the colorful balls a girl—
half-vanished like a saint
ascending heaven
—strokes her sister's brow.
The room collapses
under crushing pressure.
Darkness. The booth
a reed basket cast upon the books.
Through nothingness
the mansion swims, trailing
long tentacles, shedding
clouds of pages in its wake.

The Swans Flew Out of the Sun

And there came out of the sun
scorpions of the air.
We shot, they fell
like sandbags. Bad idea.
More came, myriads
blocking the light
like one bird. One thunder-
cloud of white feathers.
So the slow swarm
drifted in. We watched
from parks & balconies.
We imposed a curfew
declared martial law
declared war. Blasted them
with antiaircraft guns.
But these were unhappy gods.
They won the city.
Years pass. Our thoughts
turn again to beauty,
to ontology. Their coming
was prophesied. To the swans
we are *zeros. Eggs.*
They stretch our necks
with their machines
made from our machines
so we do not seem
so squat, so hideous.
We are never out of view.
Their eyes, a dot-hoard,

surveil us in our rooms
from wallpaper cracks.
I visit my lover, kiss him,
mouth full of feathers & blood
& he is at the open window
leaning. I breathe the swans
in dreams, shrouded in feathers,
shit on my skin.
They do not tolerate talk.
We *zeros* are taught
to bleat & honk. We *eggs*
honk our car horns
to inaugurate their daily fête.
We march in the fête
in white plumage.
If we cry or laugh or talk
they tear off
our lovely feathers
& we peck the bald ones
to death.

Deus Ex Machina

Viktor didn't hear them knocking.
The second toe of his left foot
had tormented him
the whole long winter,
& his earlobes ached.
How he suffered. Teeth-
grinding pain. *Schmerzhaft.*
He spilled the Roxicodone pills,
slipping face-first into
his salad. Almond dressing,
that smell. Zyklon B,
the camp. (Violent knocking.)
He'd worked in a lab.
Mixed toxic agents,
sealed grayblue pellets
in gas cans. Buried bodies.
Not that he'd forgot. Just,
he admired the man
facing the tank at Tiananmen
& somehow over time
transposed himself
onto him. The thought
of himself alone facing that machine
gave him a prideful chill.
That's when his door burst in
with a hollow *pop*
(even he heard). Large men
glided like dancers,
gelatin capsule pills
snapping under their shoes.

Before Viktor could move,
his roof creaked open
like a dollhouse.
The men, too, looked up.
From a black dot in the sky
a mechanical crane
or a dragon—some beast,
brick hide, guard tower eyes,
barbwire wings—
lurched down,
crisscrossing the blue,
scooping Viktor up
in its jaws,
& vanished into the void
above Minnesota.

On the Curiously Sinister Hearts of Donkeys

You should not have cut off the donkey's head.
That seems sure. Hard to recall
but there it lies—floppy ears,
lolling tongue—by the shucked corn
on this country road. A gory
diving helmet. The body a heap beside it,
stripes painted across the back
to look like a zebra! You put down
the machete, lift the head, appraising it.
Is it hollow? You place your head
inside it. Then the donkey thoughts begin.
You are braying rhetoric to the multitudes.
They stamp & stamp their hooves
on cobblestones as you squint, shaking
your mane. How grandiloquent you are
in your swanky uniform cluttered
with medallions. You call out to them
for favors, for their very souls
& the souls of their daughters.
You turn away. Your suspicion
grows. Teachers are ruiners.
Lovers saboteurs. *To the glue factory*
with them all! You confide only
in the stuffed human head on the wall.
This makes sense. Your loyal servant
is an elegant ass named Rahul.
Here he is! He clip-clops in,
a long-handled bucket of brandy
between his teeth. He pours it—

with great difficulty, spilling most
—into a silver trough, for you.
His last duty of each day. Rahul
clip-clops down a red staircase.
In the servants' quarters he removes
his fine collar & halter & stands
before the many mirrors naked.
He is muscular. His fur shines.
Between his hooves, a vial of arsenic.
"A wise donkey," he brays,
"does at once what a jackass does later."
His eyes, cruel, repeat infinitely.

Utøya

You have sung us down.
Middle of the island you whispered
the treasure-bearing goblin song, then howled it.
To escape the lines, some held their ears,
some gnashed their teeth, some ran,
some drowned swimming out of earshot.
Humans can enact nightmares
conceived by gods. Hatred whirls across the earth
like the polluted sea gyres. Some *draug*,
lonely demon craving an ally,
slid a thorn in your side, deep, below the ribs,
a life-in-death wound. Pawn,
you were implanted in a uterus.
Out of the Navel of Heaven you emerged,
kid with a fucked-up plan in his overalls,
scrawled by a god of war.
You were a virgin pharaoh limping the desert
in a coat of snarling dogs;
a grim princess crushing a serpent
between your fingers, gathering venom
in a bowl; a physicist haunted
by an atom humming under a microscope.
You fled to the bawds of the valley.
You appealed to the progenies of chaos.
None could remove the thorn.
One day you woke singing the hemorrhaging song,
as if it were yours; the *Mein Kampf* song;
the scratching-at-the-door-at-four-a.m.
song; the sandman-over-your-bed song
of the tongue-tied wound in your side,

which choked the kid with the deaf sister
at five in the afternoon. Your song suffocated
the kid with head lice; smothered
the pumpkin pie eater; asphyxiated
the kid with the ham radio;
strangled the kid with the potty mouth;
throttled the cigarette smoker put back a year
whose mother keeps ending up
you-know-where; gagged the girls
too young to kiss who had never kissed.
You sang us down in the sunlit forest
while golden plovers sang. You sang us down
in the fresh cut grass. Time is a skull
with a shattered jaw the wind wails through.
Bodies were hauled out by searchlight.
I cannot look at the white sheets laid across them.
A few stumbled from caves, shivering,
humming the tune, petrified.
I would like to sing your magic backwards.

Infinite Grief Song

Violet Mary sees herself
in the window
over the dishes.
Outside, a swing set.
Steam reveals
an apparitional mess,
prints on the glass.
Her dripping hands *groan*.
No, an ambulance.
No, an ice cream truck.
Behind a lamp, on the wall,
a secret smear.
Fingerprint. Ambush
of a ghost. That shadow
is wearing overalls.
Put your palms
on your eyes. Pour yourself
a glass of Tang.
O for a silver-tongued
vacuum sales guy.
She'd answer the door nude
under a fur coat.
She passes herself
on the stairs.
Spectral hausfrau!
Bright as a penny.
These weeks she dreams
moths nibble her edges.
Breasts & toes in tatters.
She holds up a palm.

Sure enough
the fingers crumble, spill,
like the last trees
in a badlands.

Last Words of the Old Man with the Photographic Memory

Born with eyes cast wide
as nets, I held earth together
with total recall.
I suffered nosebleeds.
I had no friends.
I was nine & unprepared
for my sister
her beauty. She is three,
I hold her tiny right hand,
we are crossing
a field. In her left hand
she holds a kite
tall as her. She stops,
mouth open: a deer
at the tree line.
The shoulder of the deer
rotting. A hole
dark & gaping
like some terrible insight.
I run with the string,
I tear her kite.
She sits in tall grass
in her green dress.
She isn't crying
or smiling, just looking
where the deer was.
Today it is winter,
night, cold on the lino.
Outside, city dogs
freeze. I am the deer.

Again, again
the kite in the sun:
blue light like veins
of the world.

Robbing a Bank & Suddenly Fingers that Gripped My Throat My Whole Life Let Go Song

I drop the money bag, Rodeo Drive falls away
under me, I see—
from behind the eyeholes
of my Trump mask—the capitán
who's been firing at us
& howling into his bullhorn,
the capitán
who now waves away a mosquito
& I step toward him
through the underbrush of rifles
calm as can be.
What has dislodged?
A huge tiredness upon us.
As if a volcano that does not exist
erupted, & what was in there
poured like ash
across Ventura Boulevard
down to San Diego.
The entire universe, hitherto divided,
is embodied all in one
imperishable pimp strolling by
in a fly purple wig.
The police walk stupefied among cars stalled
like a field of radioactive logs
without beginning or end. Am I dead?
I am not dead.
We drop our masks by the interstate
& walk the marshalling yards
past the choking fences of Santa Barbara
to the desert.

There is a hot wind from Tijuana.
Both sides stopped firing
over the border.
As when the world
was young, when every living thing
was blind.
The worm demanded nothing.
There isn't even any need
to glorify the good.

Last Book of the Last Library on Earth

A heavy iron volume burst out
a stained glass window
to the stones at our feet.
A scholar plunged after.
Our brothers of the light guns
& clear shields
spattlecocked him.
I fought to the bloodbright book,
my fingers knives
& I took it. I did not
behave well. Odd.
You will never know
of this day. Records
purged. The functionaries
started the clocks again
at zero, as promised.
But I had it, *boc, bokiz, bōk,*
colossal blood testimony.
Proof. I staggered away
in the kiln of dusk clutching it
like a balsa raft
to my kitchen table,
opening at a page
of closed loops, scrivened:
VIVIANS, A DEAD RACE.
Lost scout on mountain pass
defecates in his hand,
shapes it as it freezes
into a knife & with it
eviscerates his dog.

Fygure 1. Lost scout
sits, fur-clad, in the dog.
Underwrit: *We're drawne*
t' whaire we ende
like snowe. The scout,
upon the corpse-
toboggan, slides to safety,
is made chieftain,
drives the tribe into
its darkest age
of butcheries & war.

The Thief

Over weeks the objects in my house began to vanish, one at a time.
Furniture, books. My cabinet of curiosities: scarified pocket watch,
two-headed goat skeleton, Abd-el-Kadir pipe, stinger without a bee.
My flea circus. Even my hairless cat. The place was bare. How'd they
get the harpsichord out the damn window? No clues were left. I had
a plan. One night I pretended to go out, then snuck back. I waited in
the shadows, a gun across my lap. After an hour the window creaked
open, as if by itself. A man stepped in. He hesitated, like a chess piece
on a square of streetlight, then glided over & sat before me. I squinted.
It was so dark. The wallpaper flowers seemed to bloom & wither &
bloom around his ears. He was beautiful. A young man—or woman
perhaps—with a high forehead. Eyes, though he frowned, deeply kind.
My heart quavered, as if rats were running under the floorboards—till
out they ran, the rats, all of them, out, out, & just like that the blind
violence, the extreme disquiet I'd felt since birth, left me. I laid down
the gun. I was crying. "Can I keep," I asked, "my fear of bridges?" He
examined his long fingers as if embarrassed. His skin gave off infini-
tesimal light, like a shoreline. "Am I absurd?" I asked. He touched my
cheek. I shut my eyes & saw the house with all its things again: I was
in bed, midsummer, nighttime, listening to the breathing beside me.
Breathing of someone I loved so much ...

The Fathers of Daisy Gertrude

Daisy limped, slow,
through the graveyard
like a ragged plague ship
in a storm. She slept
under a flowering tree
beside her scream
which remained quiet.
The stray cats
that slept on headstones
padded in & out
of her dreams. She fed them.
Daisy liked the sullen
nurses walking past,
smoking, in their mint scrubs
& white sneakers.
She wished them the luck
of the tree. One Friday,
drunk kids beat Daisy up.
She crawled to her tree
to heal. She lay there
knowing suddenly
that the tumor in her thigh
was her father at the gate
looking in. *Other* fathers
were coming, too. Razor-thin fathers
from the Nile Delta
from the towers of Saigon
frogging & worming
& spidering toward Daisy
across cities, fields, freeways

with their biblical eyes
napalm under their nails
to the graveyard gate
to be near Daisy
beneath her tree
where cats no longer came.
It was a night like a row
of empty mirrors.
In the day's first mists
summer leaves spread their robes.
Daisy waited, crosslegged,
breathing, till at last
the fathers scaled the gate
to pirouette in the grass:
curling, electric blue
flames.

I Am a Cell

I am a cell,
kicking out
like an old man.
The world mouth opens
into suburbs,
into harmonies.
I scream in the arms
of an island
in a blouse
of peacock feathers.
I crawl off
empty-handed.
They take names.
We stand in rows.
A girl drifts the sidewalk
on one roller skate,
calls my fingers
tapered. "Never seen
such tapered fingers,"
she says. That
enters like a hypodermic.
You can feel it going in.
I pass exams.
I grow a moustache.
Like magnets
those I love
repel each other.
She stays. We live
on a mountain.

It is quiet. Donkeys bear
the immense quiet.
One evening
as we walk uphill
holding hands,
a green apple
rolls down
past the donkeys.
From the amphitheater
of mountains
Death steps out
like a traveler.
I know Death's voice,
that oceanic hiss,
that deep *tuuung*,
like a hammer
on a muffled bell.
There is a standoff
between a honey salesman
& a dog. I release
her hand. My first grade
teacher whispers,
"Don't go out
in the snow
without your jacket."

The Prince with No Asshole

They kept him in the dark
about the dark
at the bottom of himself.
Courtiers swaddled the prince
in silk diapers. His flatus
they called "sovereign
thunder," an omen
portending good weather.
As he defecated
they trotted in a children's choir
that sang dulcetly
of the prince's glory,
right up in his face.
The priest explained,
how degraded
what ill-breeding
to ever touch *down there*.
(Just one of many
spaces, like the dungeon
& the War Room,
to distract him from.)
Perhaps he was not
the smartest prince.
As an adult he turned cruel.
From his balcony,
as the crowd below
applauded him, the prince
held his nose & cried,
"They *excrete* what they eat?

How *gauche!*" & fired
a ruby-studded musket
into the throng.
One boy in his retinue
had eyes like lanterns
on the boat of the dead.
The prince dreamt of him.
He summoned the boy
to his bedchamber.
Out of the dark stone hall
the boy came naked
bearing a horned candelabra.
The prince let him
remove his gown,
even his imperial diaper.
The boy kissed him,
tenderly. The prince
stared out the window
in a reverie. The boy
slipped a finger
into the royal anus—
the prince ejaculated at once.
Then he called out,
"Off with his head!"
At the execution
the prince was heard to say,
"One as pure as me
should never love."

Cuthbert's Plan

I followed Cuthbert's plan to a T.
We caught our breath
at the tree line
near the perimeter wall
in sackcloth masks.
Cuthbert's neck smeared
in guard blood.
Next: run like hell,
meet on the Oxen Road
at dawn. I ran until
I couldn't hear the hounds.
Slept beside a carcass
of I don't know what.
Woke running.
A megaphone roared,
"Sweet dreams till
sunbeams find you ...
Dream a little dream of me ..."
Baritone of the barbarous
Velvet Munderville.
Bees & bullets hummed
at the river. I stumbled
on a scarecrow, wrinkled,
purple. Cuthbert.
Guards circled me,
shotguns up. I crossed myself.
Shut my eyes. Opened
my eyes. Munderville
was leaning on his shotgun,
staring up at the sky.

The Great Hole had expanded.
A waterfall of stars
& darkness poured out of it
into the azure
like confetti. Bright soot
drizzled upon us.
A bloodhound floated
sideways past my ear.
Munderville smiled
in wonder. "I grew up
yonder," he said.
He coughed. A static hum
rose out of the swamp.
"Sat in this here spot
with my dog."
"I feel light in the middle,"
I said. He nodded.
We were holding
each other's shoulders.
We were choking.
"I stared at ... this sky
with awe," he said,
"... as if that made me
worthy." Just then
the weight that tore me
from the others
when I was born
vanished
& the sun became black.

Crow & Fox in Love

Fox beat Crow
with a club, dragged Crow
by the feathers.
Fox raped Crow.
Crow lopped off their own breast,
shot arrows at Fox.
Fox broke the arrows,
spit on Crow,
called Crow a *myth*.
Crow's pleasure
was a spilling cup,
so Fox sewed Crow's pleasure up.
Crow waved
a crocheted flag of Crow,
which Fox burned.
Crow heard voices ordering,
"Fight, Crow, fight!"
Fox gave such resistance a name,
a school of thought
Crow was forbidden
to learn about.
Fox tied Crow to a stake.
Roasted & cannibalized
Crow & wrote stories about it,
allegories:
Crow—enamored with Fox,
lost without Fox—
jumps in front of a train;
swallows ratsbane;

stabs self with a dagger, &c.
Crow stormed out,
slammed the door.
"Why," said Fox,
"do you not behave?
Can't you accept an apology?"

Rear Window

After the trauma
I convalesced in my flat
limping to & fro
smoking nickel cigars
& spying on my neighbors
with binoculars.
There was this one
fat, hairy dude.
I watched him 24/7,
sure he'd commit
a crime soon.
Then one evening
before my eyes
he cut his father's head off.
"I knew it!" I cried.
At that moment
my girlfriend
who is beyond gorgeous
steps in. She wears
a Paris dress, a pearl necklace,
& she is kissing me.
I tell her about
the homicidal neighbor.
I wag my finger
& yell. I'm really
getting into it.
She pats my head.
"My love," she says,
"*you* are a whale
far out in the ocean,

singing at a pitch
different from the rest."
"Thanks," I say,
"but *he* is a killer,
a parricide!" Her fingers
are in my hair.
"When one such as you
is crushed by misfortune,
they turn beautiful."
"Look!" I shout, "There!
Now he is murdering
his own child ..."
"Sweetheart,"
she laughs, "that child
has been murdered
over & over & over again
since time began.
The child will not ever
stop being murdered.
Now can we talk
about your smile?"

The Last Death

It had all happened before. The teacup
with the ship on it, steaming on the windowsill.
Their handholding at dusk, coyotes barking
in the forest. This was the transfiguration, the last,
the turn. He would not get another turn.
After this *he* would be the ancestor—
from whom later forms evolve, later souls
—who does not come back. These were, he knew,
his last moments to love her.
He pressed the thin bones of her hand.
Their story had begun in walking
shaggy, gnomic, bent
across a cracked desert. They buried
each other. He was the one
with the tendency to cling.
She wandered, overseeing her acres,
returning epochs later
in one form or another. Once
waving to him on a chain gang
as a bearded man. This time
stepping out of the forest by his shack
like a sibyl in a trance.
He will always try this hard,
she thought. Wrong. Now & never again
he watched her. Their soft table talk
echoed. I will carry her voice to the next place,
he thought. But of course he could not.
Already the Sirens were singing,
lyrics smothered by the wind.

As she slept he slipped out, removing
his shoes & pants & shirt & rings
& her flame like an amulet at his neck,
& followed the melody into the shadows.

This This is the End

And when and when my snaggletooth wife
Backs out of the driveway beside a grinning fool
I think this this is the end
I drive all night I run over a cat
Her kitten clawing scrabbling blind in the dirt
I scoop her up she purrs
In the hook of my arm for a year
And when and when
My mother my impossibly kind mother
Holds an X-ray of her skull
Her finger upon a crabapple lump
And she no longer talks and she hums
That is no song I say and her eyes are stones
I think this this must be the end
I speak to the ocean at dusk
I say Dear Ocean am I not the worst thing
The spinning world has ever made
The waves drink my hair
The waves urge me like a leaf to my bed
And when and when I am kissed by a bus
The crystal bowl of my ribcage
Bursts and the ripened fruit within it
Burns to fossil and to ash
My father stands in a forest a Vicodin moon above
And my few close ones hold hands
And when and when a war erupts
For the water of my country
And survivors encamp in the ruins of malls
Thawing their souls at bonfires of books
Still the women walk slow

To the virulent river the rapturous river
To wash their hair at dawn
And when and when the last bird shuts its eyes
And the flesh of the last whale
Drifts like pollen in turquoise ink
And dust devils are lords of the squares
And trees reclaim the stairs
Still the stars glister like sparklers
Aloft in the hand of a girl
Still the earth our grave hurdles with grace in the dark

ACKNOWLEDGMENTS

My thanks to the editors of publications in which the following poems first appeared:

American Poetry Review: "This This is the End"; *The Antigonish Review*: "Having Read *The Book of Coming Forth by Day* ...," "The Two-Headed House," and "I Am a Cell"; *Arc*: "Ash Baptism"; *Atlanta Review*: "The Bureaucrats"; *Border Crossings*: "My Houseguest"; *Borderlands: Texas Poetry Review*: "Penitentiary"; *The Cincinnati Review*: "Your Suitors"; *CV2*: "The Last Death"; *Event*: "Rear Window"; *Freefall*: "The Wonderful Hat"; *Grain*: "Hammer"; *Hotel Amerika*: "A Scorneful Image or Monstrus Shape ..."; *Lake Effect*: "The Fathers of Daisy Gertrude"; *Literary Matters*: "A Briefe & Marveyllous Hystory of Franklin"; *The Malahat Review*: "Utøya"; *Mudlark*: "The Death of Jolly Dolly"; *POOL*: "The Confession of Chunosuke Matsuyama"; *Prairie Fire*: "Urgent Message from the Captain of the Unicorn Hunters"; *PRISM*: "Last Words of the Old Man with the Photographic Memory"; *The Puritan*: "The Prince with No Asshole" and "Crow & Fox in Love"; *The SHOp*: "Voyeur"; *The Stinging Fly*: "Tale of the Boy & the Horse Head"; *Vallum*: "The Swans Flew Out of the Sun"; *The Winnipeg Review*: "On the Curiously Sinister Hearts of Donkeys."

"Urgent Message from the Captain of the Unicorn Hunters" was included in *Best Canadian Poetry 2015* (Tightrope Books, 2015) and *Best of the Best Canadian Poetry* (Tightrope Books, 2017). I am grateful to Molly Peacock, Anita Lahey and Jacob McArthur Mooney for that.

Many thanks to the judges of The Montreal International Poetry Prize for shortlisting "The Stiltwalkers" (2011) and "The Problem with Love" (2013), and for including them in respective editions of their *Global Poetry Anthology* (Véhicule Press).

Many thanks to Australian journal *Going Down Swinging* (in collaboration with *PRISM*) for republishing "Last Words of the Old Man with the Photographic Memory" on their website, and to *PRISM* for making that poem one of their 2017 National Magazine Award submissions.

My gratitude to the Canada Council for the Arts, and to the Nova Scotia Department of Tourism, Culture and Heritage, for assistance during crucial stages in the development of this book.

For their friendship and encouragement and editorial suggestions, warm thanks to Stephanie Bolster, Micheline Maylor, Nanci Lee, Stephanie Yorke, Cory Lavender, Kyle Brown-Watson, Kate Rogers, Ben Gallagher, Blair Reeve, Brian Bartlett, Tonja Gunvaldsen Klaassen, George Elliott Clarke, and Jeremy McCormack.

Many thanks to Don McKay, John Glenday, and all the beautiful participants at the 2010 Banff Writing Studio, where the seed of this book cracked and took hold.

Many thanks to Palimpsest Press—especially Aimée Parent Dunn, Jim Johnstone, and Dawn Kresan—for doing this with me a fourth time.

And to my mother, Jean, who emails me exclamation marks every time I get a poem published.

And to Tiina, the love of my life.

ABOUT THE AUTHOR

John Wall Barger's poems have appeared in *American Poetry Review*, *Rattle*, *The Cincinnati Review*, *Poetry Ireland Review*, and *Best of the Best Canadian Poetry*. His third collection, *The Book of Festus* (Palimpsest), was a finalist for the 2016 J.M. Abraham Poetry Award. His poem, "Smog Mother," was co-winner of the *Malahat Review*'s 2017 Long Poem Prize. He lives in Philadelphia, and is an editor for *Painted Bride Quarterly*.

PHOTO CREDIT: JEREMY MCCORMACK